# 50 Premium Breakfast and Brunch Dishes

By: Kelly Johnson

# Table of Contents

- Lobster Benedict
- Smoked Salmon and Avocado Toast
- Truffle Scrambled Eggs
- Croissant French Toast with Berries
- Eggs Florentine with Hollandaise Sauce
- Shakshuka with Feta and Herbs
- Crab Cakes with Poached Eggs
- Duck Confit Hash with Poached Eggs
- Sweet Potato Hash with Chorizo
- Ricotta Pancakes with Maple Syrup
- Brioche Cinnamon Rolls
- Wild Mushroom Omelette
- Baked Eggs with Spinach and Parmesan
- Avocado and Poached Egg Tartine
- Quiche Lorraine with a Puff Pastry Crust
- Stuffed Crepes with Fresh Fruit
- Grilled Peach and Burrata Salad
- Smoked Salmon Bagel with Cream Cheese
- Chia Seed Pudding with Mango
- Lemon Ricotta Pancakes with Blueberry Compote
- Charcuterie Board with Pastries
- Clam Chowder Breakfast Biscuits
- Sourdough Waffles with Whipped Cream
- Truffle Mac and Cheese with Bacon
- Huevos Rancheros with Guacamole
- Banana Foster French Toast
- Spicy Shakshuka with Harissa
- Coconut French Toast with Passionfruit Syrup
- Avocado Toast with Poached Egg and Microgreens
- Cinnamon Sugar Doughnuts
- Blue Cornmeal Pancakes with Agave Butter
- Mediterranean Frittata with Kalamata Olives and Feta
- Soft-Shell Crab Benedict
- Salmon Roe and Avocado Salad
- Brioche Benedict with Braised Short Ribs

- Black Truffle Quiche
- Smoked Salmon Hash with Fresh Herbs
- Coconut Yogurt Parfait with Granola and Berries
- Duck and Waffle with Maple Syrup
- Eggs Benedict with Crab and Asparagus
- Avocado and Bacon Deviled Eggs
- Buttermilk Biscuits with Sausage Gravy
- Pecan Crusted French Toast
- Churros with Chocolate Sauce
- Poached Pears with Ricotta
- Lemon Poppy Seed Muffins
- Sausage and Mushroom Breakfast Casserole
- Baked Avocado with Egg
- Mango and Coconut Smoothie Bowl
- Sweet Ricotta Croissants with Lemon Zest

Lobster Benedict:

**Ingredients:**

- 2 lobster tails
- 4 English muffin halves, toasted
- 4 large eggs
- 1 tablespoon white vinegar
- 1 tablespoon butter
- 1/2 cup hollandaise sauce (store-bought or homemade)
- Fresh chives, chopped (for garnish)
- Salt and pepper, to taste
- Paprika (optional, for garnish)

**For Hollandaise Sauce:**

- 3 large egg yolks
- 1/2 cup unsalted butter, melted
- 1 tablespoon fresh lemon juice
- 1 teaspoon Dijon mustard
- Salt and cayenne pepper, to taste

**Instructions:**

1. **Cook the Lobster:**
    - Bring a pot of water to a boil. Add salt and drop in the lobster tails. Boil for about 6-8 minutes, or until the shells are bright red and the meat is opaque. Remove the lobster, let it cool slightly, and then remove the meat from the shells. Chop the lobster meat into bite-sized pieces. Set aside.
2. **Prepare the Hollandaise Sauce:**
    - In a heatproof bowl, whisk together the egg yolks, lemon juice, Dijon mustard, salt, and cayenne pepper.
    - Place the bowl over a saucepan of simmering water (double boiler method). Whisk constantly, adding melted butter in a slow stream until the sauce thickens. Adjust seasoning to taste, then remove from heat and keep warm.
3. **Poach the Eggs:**
    - Fill a saucepan with water and add a tablespoon of white vinegar. Bring to a gentle simmer.

- Crack the eggs into small bowls or cups. Gently slide each egg into the simmering water. Poach for about 3-4 minutes or until the whites are set but the yolks remain soft. Remove the eggs with a slotted spoon and drain on a paper towel.

4. **Assemble the Benedict:**
    - Place two toasted English muffin halves on each plate. Spoon the lobster meat over the muffin halves.
    - Carefully place a poached egg on top of the lobster.
    - Drizzle with warm hollandaise sauce and sprinkle with chopped chives and paprika for garnish.

5. **Serve:**
    - Serve immediately and enjoy your luxurious Lobster Benedict!

## Smoked Salmon and Avocado Toast

**Ingredients:**

- 2 slices of sourdough bread or whole-grain bread
- 1 ripe avocado
- 4 oz smoked salmon
- 1 tablespoon lemon juice
- 1 tablespoon olive oil
- Salt and pepper, to taste
- Fresh dill, for garnish
- Red onion slices (optional)

**Instructions:**

1. **Toast the Bread:**
    - Toast the slices of bread until golden and crispy.
2. **Prepare the Avocado:**
    - In a small bowl, mash the avocado with lemon juice, olive oil, salt, and pepper. Adjust seasoning to taste.
3. **Assemble the Toast:**
    - Spread the mashed avocado evenly over the toasted bread slices.
    - Top with smoked salmon, red onion slices (if desired), and garnish with fresh dill.
4. **Serve:**
    - Serve immediately for a fresh and delicious breakfast or snack.

## Truffle Scrambled Eggs

**Ingredients:**

- 4 large eggs
- 1 tablespoon butter
- 1 tablespoon truffle oil (or truffle butter)
- Salt and pepper, to taste
- Fresh chives, chopped (for garnish)
- Grated Parmesan (optional)

**Instructions:**

1. **Whisk the Eggs:**
    - In a bowl, whisk the eggs with a pinch of salt and pepper until smooth and well combined.
2. **Cook the Scrambled Eggs:**
    - Heat the butter in a non-stick skillet over medium-low heat.
    - Pour in the eggs and cook slowly, stirring gently with a spatula to form soft curds.
3. **Add Truffle Oil:**
    - Once the eggs are almost done, drizzle the truffle oil over them and stir to incorporate.
4. **Finish and Serve:**
    - Garnish with fresh chives and grated Parmesan (if using). Serve immediately with toasted bread or a side of greens.

**Croissant French Toast with Berries**

**Ingredients:**

- 2 croissants (preferably a day or two old)
- 2 large eggs
- 1/2 cup milk or heavy cream
- 1 tablespoon vanilla extract
- 1 tablespoon cinnamon (optional)
- 2 tablespoons butter
- 1 cup mixed berries (strawberries, blueberries, raspberries)
- Maple syrup, for drizzling
- Powdered sugar, for garnish

**Instructions:**

1. **Prepare the Egg Mixture:**
   - In a shallow bowl, whisk together the eggs, milk, vanilla, and cinnamon (if using).
2. **Slice the Croissants:**
   - Slice the croissants in half horizontally.
3. **Dip and Cook the Croissants:**
   - Heat butter in a skillet over medium heat.
   - Dip each croissant half into the egg mixture, coating both sides, and place in the skillet. Cook for 2-3 minutes per side, until golden brown and crispy.
4. **Assemble the French Toast:**
   - Stack the croissant halves on plates, top with fresh berries, and drizzle with maple syrup.
5. **Serve:**
   - Dust with powdered sugar and serve immediately for a sweet and indulgent breakfast.

# Eggs Florentine with Hollandaise Sauce

## Ingredients:

- 2 English muffins, split and toasted
- 4 large eggs
- 2 cups spinach, sautéed
- 2 tbsp butter
- 1/2 cup hollandaise sauce (store-bought or homemade)
- Fresh parsley, chopped (for garnish)
- Salt and pepper, to taste

## Instructions:

1. **Poach the Eggs:**
    - In a saucepan of simmering water with a tablespoon of vinegar, poach the eggs for 3-4 minutes until the whites are set and yolks are runny.
2. **Prepare the Spinach:**
    - Sauté the spinach in butter until wilted. Season with salt and pepper.
3. **Assemble:**
    - Place the toasted muffin halves on plates. Top with a spoonful of sautéed spinach, followed by a poached egg.
    - Drizzle with hollandaise sauce and garnish with fresh parsley.
4. **Serve:**
    - Serve immediately for a classic and luxurious breakfast.

# Shakshuka with Feta and Herbs

## Ingredients:

- 2 tbsp olive oil
- 1 onion, chopped
- 1 bell pepper, chopped
- 2 cloves garlic, minced
- 1 can (14 oz) diced tomatoes
- 1 tsp ground cumin
- 1 tsp paprika
- 1/2 tsp chili flakes (optional)
- 4 large eggs
- 1/2 cup feta cheese, crumbled
- Fresh parsley and cilantro, chopped
- Salt and pepper, to taste

## Instructions:

1. **Sauté the Vegetables:**
   - Heat olive oil in a skillet over medium heat. Sauté onion, bell pepper, and garlic until soft and fragrant.
2. **Add Tomatoes and Spices:**
   - Stir in diced tomatoes, cumin, paprika, and chili flakes. Simmer for 10-15 minutes, letting the sauce thicken.
3. **Add the Eggs:**
   - Make wells in the sauce and crack the eggs into each well. Cover and cook for 6-8 minutes, until the eggs are cooked to your liking.
4. **Garnish and Serve:**
   - Sprinkle with crumbled feta and fresh herbs. Serve with warm pita bread.

# Crab Cakes with Poached Eggs

## Ingredients:

- 1 lb crab meat
- 1/2 cup breadcrumbs
- 2 tbsp mayonnaise
- 1 tbsp Dijon mustard
- 1 egg, beaten
- 1 tbsp parsley, chopped
- 1 tbsp lemon juice
- 4 large eggs (for poaching)
- Salt and pepper, to taste
- Olive oil for frying

## Instructions:

1. **Make Crab Cakes:**
   - Mix crab meat, breadcrumbs, mayonnaise, mustard, beaten egg, parsley, lemon juice, salt, and pepper. Form into 4 cakes.
2. **Cook the Crab Cakes:**
   - Heat olive oil in a skillet over medium heat. Cook crab cakes for 4-5 minutes on each side, until golden and crispy.
3. **Poach the Eggs:**
   - Poach the eggs in simmering water for 3-4 minutes.
4. **Assemble:**
   - Place a crab cake on each plate and top with a poached egg.
5. **Serve:**
   - Serve immediately with hollandaise or a drizzle of lemon for a decadent brunch.

# Duck Confit Hash with Poached Eggs

## Ingredients:

- 2 duck confit legs, shredded
- 2 medium potatoes, diced
- 1 onion, chopped
- 1 red bell pepper, chopped
- 1 tbsp olive oil
- 2 large eggs (for poaching)
- Salt and pepper, to taste
- Fresh herbs, chopped

## Instructions:

1. **Make the Hash:**
   - Heat olive oil in a large skillet. Sauté potatoes, onion, and bell pepper until golden and tender. Add shredded duck confit and cook until heated through.
2. **Poach the Eggs:**
   - Poach eggs in simmering water for 3-4 minutes.
3. **Assemble and Serve:**
   - Serve the hash topped with poached eggs and garnish with fresh herbs.

# Sweet Potato Hash with Chorizo

## Ingredients:

- 2 medium sweet potatoes, peeled and diced
- 1 chorizo sausage, casings removed
- 1 red onion, chopped
- 1 bell pepper, chopped
- 2 tbsp olive oil
- Salt and pepper, to taste
- Fresh cilantro, for garnish

## Instructions:

1. **Cook the Chorizo:**
    - Heat olive oil in a skillet. Cook chorizo, breaking it up with a spoon, until browned and cooked through.
2. **Cook the Vegetables:**
    - Add diced sweet potatoes, onion, and bell pepper. Cook until tender and caramelized, about 10-12 minutes.
3. **Serve:**
    - Serve the hash topped with a poached or fried egg and garnish with fresh cilantro.

# Ricotta Pancakes with Maple Syrup

## Ingredients:

- 1 cup ricotta cheese
- 1 cup all-purpose flour
- 2 large eggs
- 1/2 cup milk
- 1/4 cup sugar
- 1 tsp vanilla extract
- 1 tsp baking powder
- Pinch of salt
- Butter, for cooking
- Maple syrup, for serving

## Instructions:

1. **Make the Pancake Batter:**
    - In a bowl, mix ricotta, eggs, milk, sugar, vanilla, flour, baking powder, and salt until smooth.
2. **Cook the Pancakes:**
    - Heat a little butter in a skillet over medium heat. Pour batter into the skillet and cook until bubbles form on the surface. Flip and cook for another 2-3 minutes.
3. **Serve:**
    - Serve the pancakes warm with maple syrup.

## Brioche Cinnamon Rolls

### Ingredients:

- 4 cups all-purpose flour
- 1/2 cup sugar
- 1/2 tsp salt
- 1 tbsp active dry yeast
- 1/2 cup milk, warm
- 1/2 cup unsalted butter, melted
- 2 large eggs
- 1 tbsp cinnamon
- 1/2 cup brown sugar
- 1 cup cream cheese frosting (optional)

### Instructions:

1. **Make the Dough:**
   - Mix flour, sugar, salt, and yeast. Add warm milk, melted butter, and eggs. Knead until smooth, then let rise for 1 hour.
2. **Make the Filling:**
   - Mix cinnamon and brown sugar. Roll dough into a rectangle, spread with butter, and sprinkle with cinnamon-sugar mixture. Roll up and cut into slices.
3. **Bake the Rolls:**
   - Place rolls in a baking dish, let rise for another 30 minutes. Bake at 350°F for 20-25 minutes.
4. **Serve:**
   - Drizzle with cream cheese frosting (optional) and serve warm.

# Wild Mushroom Omelette

## Ingredients:

- 4 large eggs
- 1/2 cup wild mushrooms, sliced
- 2 tbsp butter
- 1/4 cup cheese (grated, optional)
- Fresh herbs (thyme, parsley), chopped
- Salt and pepper, to taste

## Instructions:

1. **Cook the Mushrooms:**
   - Sauté mushrooms in butter until tender and browned.
2. **Make the Omelette:**
   - Whisk eggs with salt and pepper. Pour into a heated skillet and cook until set, adding mushrooms and cheese in the center. Fold and cook for another 1-2 minutes.
3. **Serve:**
   - Garnish with fresh herbs and serve hot.

# Baked Eggs with Spinach and Parmesan

## Ingredients:

- 4 large eggs
- 2 cups fresh spinach
- 1/2 cup Parmesan cheese, grated
- 2 tbsp butter
- Salt and pepper, to taste

## Instructions:

1. **Sauté Spinach:**
   - Sauté spinach in butter until wilted. Season with salt and pepper.
2. **Bake the Eggs:**
   - Place spinach in a baking dish, make wells, and crack eggs into the wells. Sprinkle with Parmesan. Bake at 375°F for 10-12 minutes, until eggs are set.
3. **Serve:**
   - Serve immediately with crusty bread.

# Avocado and Poached Egg Tartine

**Ingredients:**

- 2 slices of sourdough or rustic bread, toasted
- 1 ripe avocado, mashed
- 2 large eggs (for poaching)
- Fresh lemon juice
- Salt and pepper, to taste
- Fresh herbs (optional, for garnish)
- Red pepper flakes (optional)

**Instructions:**

1. **Prepare the Tartine:**
   - Spread mashed avocado on the toasted bread slices. Squeeze a little lemon juice over the top, and season with salt and pepper.
2. **Poach the Eggs:**
   - Poach eggs in simmering water for 3-4 minutes until the whites are set and yolks are runny.
3. **Assemble the Tartine:**
   - Place a poached egg on top of each avocado toast. Sprinkle with fresh herbs and red pepper flakes (optional).
4. **Serve:**
   - Serve immediately as a fresh, nutritious breakfast or light lunch.

# Quiche Lorraine with a Puff Pastry Crust

## Ingredients:

- 1 puff pastry sheet (store-bought)
- 1/2 lb bacon, cooked and crumbled
- 1/2 cup grated Gruyère cheese
- 1/2 cup heavy cream
- 3 large eggs
- 1/4 tsp nutmeg
- Salt and pepper, to taste
- 1/2 cup milk
- 1 small onion, finely chopped

## Instructions:

1. **Prepare the Puff Pastry:**
    - Preheat oven to 375°F (190°C). Fit the puff pastry into a tart pan or pie dish. Prick the bottom with a fork and bake for 10-12 minutes, until golden.
2. **Make the Filling:**
    - In a bowl, whisk together eggs, heavy cream, milk, nutmeg, salt, and pepper. Stir in crumbled bacon, cheese, and onions.
3. **Assemble and Bake:**
    - Pour the egg mixture into the pre-baked crust. Bake for 30-35 minutes, or until the quiche is set and golden on top.
4. **Serve:**
    - Let cool slightly before serving.

## Stuffed Crepes with Fresh Fruit

### Ingredients:

- 8 crepes (store-bought or homemade)
- 1 cup ricotta cheese
- 1/2 cup mascarpone cheese
- 1 tbsp honey
- 1 tsp vanilla extract
- Fresh berries (strawberries, blueberries, raspberries)
- Fresh mint leaves (optional, for garnish)

### Instructions:

1. **Prepare the Filling:**
    - In a bowl, mix ricotta, mascarpone, honey, and vanilla until smooth.
2. **Assemble the Crepes:**
    - Spread a spoonful of the filling onto each crepe and fold them into quarters.
3. **Serve:**
    - Top with fresh fruit and garnish with mint leaves. Serve immediately.

## Grilled Peach and Burrata Salad

### Ingredients:

- 2 ripe peaches, halved and pitted
- 1 tbsp olive oil
- Salt and pepper, to taste
- 4 oz burrata cheese
- Arugula or mixed greens
- 1 tbsp balsamic glaze
- Fresh basil, chopped

### Instructions:

1. **Grill the Peaches:**
    - Heat a grill pan over medium-high heat. Brush peach halves with olive oil, season with salt and pepper, and grill for 2-3 minutes per side, until slightly charred.
2. **Assemble the Salad:**
    - Place grilled peaches on a plate, add a scoop of burrata cheese, and arrange arugula or mixed greens around it.
3. **Finish and Serve:**
    - Drizzle with balsamic glaze and sprinkle with fresh basil. Serve immediately.

# Smoked Salmon Bagel with Cream Cheese

## Ingredients:

- 2 bagels, halved and toasted
- 4 oz cream cheese
- 4 oz smoked salmon, thinly sliced
- 1 small red onion, thinly sliced
- Fresh dill, chopped
- Lemon wedges

## Instructions:

1. **Prepare the Bagels:**
    - Spread a generous layer of cream cheese on each toasted bagel half.
2. **Assemble the Bagel:**
    - Top with smoked salmon, red onion slices, and fresh dill.
3. **Serve:**
    - Serve with lemon wedges on the side for a refreshing citrus squeeze.

# Chia Seed Pudding with Mango

## Ingredients:

- 1/2 cup chia seeds
- 1 1/2 cups coconut milk (or almond milk)
- 1 tbsp honey or maple syrup
- 1 tsp vanilla extract
- 1 ripe mango, peeled and diced

## Instructions:

1. **Make the Chia Pudding:**
     - In a bowl, whisk together chia seeds, coconut milk, honey, and vanilla. Let sit in the fridge for at least 2 hours or overnight, stirring occasionally.
2. **Serve:**
     - Spoon the chia pudding into bowls and top with fresh mango.

# Lemon Ricotta Pancakes with Blueberry Compote

## Ingredients:

- 1 cup ricotta cheese
- 1 cup all-purpose flour
- 2 large eggs
- 1/2 cup milk
- 1 tbsp lemon zest
- 1 tbsp sugar
- 1 tsp baking powder
- Pinch of salt
- 1 cup blueberries
- 1/4 cup water
- 1 tbsp honey

## Instructions:

1. **Make the Pancakes:**
    - Whisk together ricotta, eggs, milk, lemon zest, sugar, flour, baking powder, and salt. Heat a skillet and cook pancakes until golden on both sides.
2. **Make the Compote:**
    - In a saucepan, heat blueberries, water, and honey. Simmer for 5-7 minutes until the berries burst and the mixture thickens.
3. **Serve:**
    - Serve the pancakes with a drizzle of blueberry compote on top.

# Charcuterie Board with Pastries

## Ingredients:

- Assorted cured meats (prosciutto, salami, chorizo)
- Cheese selection (brie, cheddar, goat cheese, blue cheese)
- Fresh fruits (grapes, figs, apples)
- Crackers and bread
- Assorted pastries (croissants, petit fours, fruit tarts)

## Instructions:

1. **Arrange the Charcuterie Board:**
   - Arrange meats, cheeses, fresh fruits, and crackers on a large board or platter.
2. **Add Pastries:**
   - Include an assortment of small pastries like croissants, fruit tarts, and petit fours.
3. **Serve:**
   - Serve the charcuterie board with wine or beverages of choice.

# Clam Chowder Breakfast Biscuits

## Ingredients:

- 1 can (6.5 oz) clam chowder, drained
- 2 cups all-purpose flour
- 1 tablespoon baking powder
- 1/2 teaspoon salt
- 1/4 teaspoon black pepper
- 1/2 cup cold butter, cubed
- 1/2 cup milk
- 1/2 cup shredded cheddar cheese
- 1/4 cup chopped fresh parsley (optional)

## Instructions:

1. **Prepare the Biscuits:**
   - Preheat the oven to 375°F (190°C). In a large bowl, whisk together flour, baking powder, salt, and pepper. Add cold butter and use a pastry cutter to cut it into the dry ingredients until it resembles coarse crumbs.
2. **Add the Wet Ingredients:**
   - Stir in the clam chowder and milk. Mix until just combined. Fold in shredded cheddar cheese and chopped parsley.
3. **Form and Bake:**
   - Drop spoonfuls of dough onto a greased baking sheet and bake for 12-15 minutes, until golden brown.
4. **Serve:**
   - Serve warm for a savory breakfast treat.

# Sourdough Waffles with Whipped Cream

## Ingredients:

- 1 cup sourdough starter (fed or unfed)
- 1 1/2 cups all-purpose flour
- 1 tablespoon sugar
- 1 teaspoon baking powder
- 1/2 teaspoon baking soda
- 1/2 teaspoon salt
- 1 large egg
- 1 cup milk
- 1/4 cup melted butter
- 1 teaspoon vanilla extract
- Whipped cream, for serving
- Fresh berries, for garnish

## Instructions:

1. **Prepare the Waffle Batter:**
    - Preheat your waffle iron. In a large bowl, mix together the sourdough starter, flour, sugar, baking powder, baking soda, and salt. In a separate bowl, whisk together the egg, milk, melted butter, and vanilla extract. Combine both mixtures and stir until just smooth.
2. **Cook the Waffles:**
    - Pour the batter into the preheated waffle iron and cook according to your iron's instructions, usually for about 3-5 minutes.
3. **Serve:**
    - Serve the waffles topped with whipped cream and fresh berries for a delicious breakfast.

# Truffle Mac and Cheese with Bacon

## Ingredients:

- 1 lb elbow macaroni
- 4 tablespoons butter
- 2 tablespoons all-purpose flour
- 2 cups whole milk
- 2 cups shredded sharp cheddar cheese
- 1/2 cup grated Parmesan cheese
- 2 tablespoons truffle oil
- 6 strips bacon, cooked and crumbled
- Salt and pepper, to taste
- Fresh parsley, chopped (for garnish)

## Instructions:

1. **Cook the Macaroni:**
   - Cook the macaroni according to package directions, then drain and set aside.
2. **Make the Cheese Sauce:**
   - In a large saucepan, melt butter over medium heat. Stir in flour and cook for 1 minute. Gradually whisk in milk and cook until the sauce thickens. Stir in cheddar cheese, Parmesan, truffle oil, and crumbled bacon. Season with salt and pepper.
3. **Combine and Serve:**
   - Add the cooked macaroni to the cheese sauce and stir until well coated. Serve garnished with fresh parsley.

# Huevos Rancheros with Guacamole

## Ingredients:

- 4 corn tortillas
- 4 large eggs
- 1/2 cup salsa (store-bought or homemade)
- 1 avocado, mashed
- 1/4 cup chopped cilantro
- 1 tablespoon lime juice
- Salt and pepper, to taste
- Olive oil, for frying

## Instructions:

1. **Fry the Tortillas:**
   - Heat a skillet over medium heat with a little olive oil. Fry each tortilla for about 1-2 minutes per side, until crispy. Set aside.
2. **Cook the Eggs:**
   - In the same skillet, cook the eggs sunny side up or to your preferred doneness.
3. **Assemble:**
   - Place a fried tortilla on each plate, top with a fried egg, and spoon salsa over the egg.
4. **Prepare the Guacamole:**
   - Mash the avocado and mix with cilantro, lime juice, salt, and pepper.
5. **Serve:**
   - Serve the huevos rancheros with a dollop of guacamole on top.

# Banana Foster French Toast

## Ingredients:

- 4 slices of thick bread (such as brioche or challah)
- 2 large eggs
- 1/2 cup milk
- 1/2 teaspoon cinnamon
- 1/4 teaspoon nutmeg
- 2 ripe bananas, sliced
- 1/4 cup brown sugar
- 1/4 cup dark rum
- 1 tablespoon butter
- Whipped cream, for topping

## Instructions:

1. **Prepare the French Toast:**
   - In a bowl, whisk together eggs, milk, cinnamon, and nutmeg. Dip each slice of bread into the egg mixture, making sure to coat both sides.
2. **Cook the French Toast:**
   - Heat a skillet over medium heat and cook the bread slices until golden brown on both sides, about 3-4 minutes per side. Remove from the skillet and set aside.
3. **Make the Banana Foster Sauce:**
   - In the same skillet, melt butter over medium heat. Add brown sugar and stir until dissolved. Add the sliced bananas and cook for 1-2 minutes. Carefully add the rum, allowing it to flame (optional), then stir until the sauce thickens.
4. **Serve:**
   - Spoon the banana foster sauce over the French toast and top with whipped cream.

# Spicy Shakshuka with Harissa

## Ingredients:

- 1 tablespoon olive oil
- 1 onion, chopped
- 1 bell pepper, chopped
- 2 cloves garlic, minced
- 1 can (14 oz) crushed tomatoes
- 2 tablespoons harissa paste
- 1 teaspoon paprika
- 1 teaspoon cumin
- 4 large eggs
- Fresh cilantro, for garnish
- Salt and pepper, to taste

## Instructions:

1. **Cook the Vegetables:**
   - Heat olive oil in a skillet over medium heat. Add onion, bell pepper, and garlic and sauté for 5 minutes until softened.
2. **Add the Sauce:**
   - Stir in crushed tomatoes, harissa, paprika, and cumin. Simmer for 10-15 minutes until the sauce thickens.
3. **Poach the Eggs:**
   - Make small wells in the sauce and crack eggs into each well. Cover the skillet and cook for about 5-7 minutes, or until the eggs are poached to your desired level of doneness.
4. **Serve:**
   - Season with salt and pepper, garnish with cilantro, and serve with crusty bread.

# Coconut French Toast with Passionfruit Syrup

## Ingredients:

- 4 slices of brioche or challah
- 1/2 cup shredded coconut
- 2 large eggs
- 1/2 cup coconut milk
- 1 teaspoon vanilla extract
- 1/4 teaspoon cinnamon
- 1/2 cup passionfruit pulp (or passionfruit syrup)
- 2 tablespoons honey
- Butter, for frying

## Instructions:

1. **Prepare the French Toast:**
   - In a bowl, whisk together eggs, coconut milk, vanilla, and cinnamon. Dip the bread slices into the mixture, coating both sides.
2. **Cook the French Toast:**
   - Heat butter in a skillet over medium heat. Fry each slice of bread until golden brown on both sides.
3. **Make the Passionfruit Syrup:**
   - In a small saucepan, combine passionfruit pulp and honey. Simmer for 5 minutes until slightly thickened.
4. **Serve:**
   - Drizzle passionfruit syrup over the coconut French toast and serve.

# Avocado Toast with Poached Egg and Microgreens

## Ingredients:

- 2 slices of whole grain or sourdough bread, toasted
- 1 ripe avocado, mashed
- 2 large eggs (for poaching)
- Microgreens, for garnish
- Salt and pepper, to taste
- Olive oil, for drizzling

## Instructions:

1. **Prepare the Toast:**
    - Spread mashed avocado on the toasted bread slices. Season with salt and pepper.
2. **Poach the Eggs:**
    - Poach the eggs in simmering water for 3-4 minutes until the whites are set and the yolks are runny.
3. **Assemble and Serve:**
    - Place a poached egg on each slice of avocado toast, drizzle with olive oil, and garnish with microgreens.

# Cinnamon Sugar Doughnuts

## Ingredients:

- 2 cups all-purpose flour
- 1 teaspoon baking powder
- 1/2 teaspoon cinnamon
- 1/4 teaspoon salt
- 1/2 cup sugar
- 1/2 cup milk
- 2 large eggs
- 1/4 cup melted butter
- 1 teaspoon vanilla extract
- 1/2 cup sugar (for coating)
- 1 tablespoon cinnamon (for coating)

## Instructions:

1. **Prepare the Doughnuts:**
   - Preheat the oven to 350°F (175°C). In a bowl, mix flour, baking powder, cinnamon, salt, and sugar. Add milk, eggs, melted butter, and vanilla. Stir until smooth.
2. **Bake the Doughnuts:**
   - Spoon the batter into a greased doughnut pan and bake for 12-15 minutes, until golden brown.
3. **Coat in Cinnamon Sugar:**
   - Mix sugar and cinnamon in a small bowl. Once the doughnuts are baked and slightly cooled, toss them in the cinnamon sugar mixture.

# Blue Cornmeal Pancakes with Agave Butter

## Ingredients:

- 1 cup blue cornmeal
- 1 cup all-purpose flour
- 1 tablespoon sugar
- 1 tablespoon baking powder
- 1/2 teaspoon salt
- 1 1/4 cups milk
- 1 large egg
- 2 tablespoons melted butter
- 1/2 cup butter, softened (for agave butter)
- 2 tablespoons agave nectar

## Instructions:

1. **Make the Pancake Batter:**
   - In a bowl, mix cornmeal, flour, sugar, baking powder, and salt. In another bowl, whisk together milk, egg, and melted butter. Combine both mixtures and stir until just combined.
2. **Cook the Pancakes:**
   - Heat a skillet over medium heat and lightly grease. Pour batter onto the skillet and cook for 2-3 minutes per side, until golden brown.
3. **Make the Agave Butter:**
   - Mix softened butter with agave nectar until smooth.
4. **Serve:**
   - Serve pancakes with agave butter on top.

# Mediterranean Frittata with Kalamata Olives and Feta

## Ingredients:

- 8 large eggs
- 1/4 cup milk
- 1/2 cup feta cheese, crumbled
- 1/4 cup Kalamata olives, sliced
- 1/4 cup sun-dried tomatoes, chopped
- 1/4 cup fresh spinach, chopped
- 1/4 teaspoon salt
- 1/4 teaspoon black pepper
- 1 tablespoon olive oil

## Instructions:

1. **Preheat the Oven:**
    - Preheat your oven to 375°F (190°C).
2. **Prepare the Frittata:**
    - In a bowl, whisk together eggs, milk, feta cheese, olives, sun-dried tomatoes, spinach, salt, and pepper.
3. **Cook the Frittata:**
    - Heat olive oil in a skillet over medium heat. Pour the egg mixture into the skillet. Let cook for 2-3 minutes until the edges start to set.
4. **Finish in the Oven:**
    - Transfer the skillet to the preheated oven and bake for 8-10 minutes, or until the eggs are set and golden brown.
5. **Serve:**
    - Slice and serve warm.

## Soft-Shell Crab Benedict

**Ingredients:**

- 2 soft-shell crabs, cleaned
- 4 English muffin halves, toasted
- 4 poached eggs
- 1/2 cup hollandaise sauce (store-bought or homemade)
- 1 tablespoon olive oil
- Fresh parsley, chopped (for garnish)

**Instructions:**

1. **Prepare the Soft-Shell Crabs:**
    - Heat olive oil in a skillet over medium-high heat. Fry the soft-shell crabs for about 3-4 minutes per side until golden and crispy.
2. **Assemble the Benedict:**
    - Place the toasted English muffin halves on plates. Top each with a fried soft-shell crab, a poached egg, and a generous spoonful of hollandaise sauce.
3. **Garnish and Serve:**
    - Garnish with fresh parsley and serve immediately.

## Salmon Roe and Avocado Salad

**Ingredients:**

- 1 avocado, diced
- 1/2 cup salmon roe (or caviar)
- 2 cups mixed greens (arugula, spinach, etc.)
- 1/4 red onion, thinly sliced
- 1 tablespoon olive oil
- 1 tablespoon lemon juice
- Salt and pepper, to taste

**Instructions:**

1. **Prepare the Salad:**
   - In a large bowl, combine mixed greens, red onion, and diced avocado.
2. **Dress the Salad:**
   - Drizzle with olive oil and lemon juice. Season with salt and pepper.
3. **Top with Salmon Roe:**
   - Gently toss to combine and top with salmon roe. Serve immediately.

## Brioche Benedict with Braised Short Ribs

### Ingredients:

- 4 slices brioche, toasted
- 2 braised short ribs, shredded
- 4 poached eggs
- 1/2 cup hollandaise sauce (store-bought or homemade)
- Fresh parsley, chopped (for garnish)

### Instructions:

1. **Prepare the Braised Short Ribs:**
   - Braise short ribs according to your favorite recipe until tender. Shred the meat once cooked.
2. **Assemble the Benedict:**
   - Place a toasted brioche slice on each plate. Top with shredded short ribs, a poached egg, and hollandaise sauce.
3. **Garnish and Serve:**
   - Garnish with chopped parsley and serve immediately.

# Black Truffle Quiche

**Ingredients:**

- 1 pre-baked pie crust
- 6 large eggs
- 1 cup heavy cream
- 1/2 cup grated Gruyère cheese
- 1/4 cup black truffle oil
- 1/4 cup chopped chives
- Salt and pepper, to taste

**Instructions:**

1. **Prepare the Quiche Filling:**
    - In a bowl, whisk together eggs, heavy cream, Gruyère cheese, truffle oil, chives, salt, and pepper.
2. **Assemble and Bake the Quiche:**
    - Pour the egg mixture into the pre-baked pie crust. Bake at 350°F (175°C) for 25-30 minutes, until the quiche is set and golden on top.
3. **Serve:**
    - Let cool slightly before slicing and serving.

## Smoked Salmon Hash with Fresh Herbs

### Ingredients:

- 2 medium potatoes, diced and boiled
- 1/2 cup smoked salmon, chopped
- 2 tablespoons olive oil
- 1 small onion, diced
- 1/4 cup fresh dill, chopped
- 2 poached eggs
- Salt and pepper, to taste

### Instructions:

1. **Prepare the Hash:**
    - Heat olive oil in a skillet over medium heat. Add onion and cook until softened. Add the boiled potatoes and cook until crispy.
2. **Add the Salmon and Herbs:**
    - Stir in the smoked salmon and fresh dill. Cook for 1-2 minutes until heated through.
3. **Assemble the Dish:**
    - Serve the hash topped with a poached egg and season with salt and pepper.

# Coconut Yogurt Parfait with Granola and Berries

## Ingredients:

- 1 cup coconut yogurt
- 1/2 cup granola
- 1/2 cup mixed berries (strawberries, blueberries, raspberries)
- Honey, for drizzling (optional)

## Instructions:

1. **Assemble the Parfait:**
    - In glasses or bowls, layer coconut yogurt, granola, and mixed berries.
2. **Serve:**
    - Drizzle with honey, if desired, and serve immediately.

# Duck and Waffle with Maple Syrup

## Ingredients:

- 2 duck breasts, cooked and sliced
- 2 waffles (store-bought or homemade)
- 1/4 cup maple syrup
- Fresh thyme, for garnish

## Instructions:

1. **Cook the Duck:**
   - Cook the duck breasts to your desired doneness and slice thinly.
2. **Assemble the Dish:**
   - Place a waffle on each plate and top with sliced duck.
3. **Serve:**
   - Drizzle with maple syrup and garnish with fresh thyme.

# Eggs Benedict with Crab and Asparagus

## Ingredients:

- 4 English muffin halves, toasted
- 4 poached eggs
- 1/2 cup crab meat
- 1/2 cup hollandaise sauce (store-bought or homemade)
- 1/2 cup steamed asparagus, chopped
- Fresh chives, chopped (for garnish)

## Instructions:

1. **Prepare the Crab and Asparagus:**
    - Steam the asparagus until tender and chop. Gently heat the crab meat.
2. **Assemble the Benedict:**
    - Place a toasted English muffin half on each plate. Top with a poached egg, crab meat, and steamed asparagus. Spoon hollandaise sauce over the top.
3. **Garnish and Serve:**
    - Garnish with fresh chives and serve immediately.

# Avocado and Bacon Deviled Eggs

## Ingredients:

- 6 hard-boiled eggs, peeled and halved
- 1 ripe avocado, mashed
- 2 slices bacon, cooked and crumbled
- 2 tablespoons mayonnaise
- 1 tablespoon Dijon mustard
- 1 teaspoon lemon juice
- Salt and pepper, to taste
- Fresh chives, chopped (for garnish)

## Instructions:

1. **Prepare the Filling:**
    - Remove the yolks from the hard-boiled eggs and place them in a bowl. Mash the yolks with the avocado, mayonnaise, Dijon mustard, and lemon juice until smooth. Season with salt and pepper.
2. **Assemble the Deviled Eggs:**
    - Spoon or pipe the avocado mixture back into the egg whites.
3. **Garnish and Serve:**
    - Top with crumbled bacon and chopped chives. Serve immediately.

# Buttermilk Biscuits with Sausage Gravy

**Ingredients:**

- **For the Biscuits:**
    - 2 cups all-purpose flour
    - 2 teaspoons baking powder
    - 1/2 teaspoon baking soda
    - 1/2 teaspoon salt
    - 1/2 cup cold unsalted butter, cubed
    - 3/4 cup buttermilk
- **For the Sausage Gravy:**
    - 1 pound breakfast sausage
    - 2 tablespoons all-purpose flour
    - 2 cups whole milk
    - Salt and pepper, to taste

**Instructions:**

1. **Make the Biscuits:**
    - Preheat your oven to 425°F (220°C). In a bowl, mix together flour, baking powder, baking soda, and salt. Cut in cold butter until the mixture resembles coarse crumbs. Stir in the buttermilk until just combined. Turn the dough out onto a floured surface, roll to 1-inch thickness, and cut into biscuits. Bake for 10-12 minutes, until golden brown.
2. **Make the Sausage Gravy:**
    - Cook the sausage in a skillet over medium heat until browned. Sprinkle with flour and cook for 1 minute. Gradually add milk, stirring until the gravy thickens. Season with salt and pepper.
3. **Serve:**
    - Split the warm biscuits and spoon sausage gravy over the top. Serve immediately.

# Pecan Crusted French Toast

## Ingredients:

- 4 slices thick bread (such as brioche or challah)
- 2 large eggs
- 1/2 cup milk
- 1 teaspoon vanilla extract
- 1/4 teaspoon cinnamon
- 1/2 cup pecans, chopped
- 1 tablespoon butter
- Maple syrup, for serving

## Instructions:

1. **Prepare the Egg Mixture:**
   - In a bowl, whisk together eggs, milk, vanilla extract, and cinnamon.
2. **Prepare the Pecans:**
   - Place the chopped pecans in a shallow dish.
3. **Cook the French Toast:**
   - Dip each slice of bread in the egg mixture, then press into the pecans. Cook in a buttered skillet over medium heat for 3-4 minutes per side until golden brown.
4. **Serve:**
   - Serve with maple syrup and enjoy.

## Churros with Chocolate Sauce

**Ingredients:**

- 1 cup water
- 2 tablespoons butter
- 1 tablespoon sugar
- 1/2 teaspoon salt
- 1 cup all-purpose flour
- 2 large eggs
- 1/4 teaspoon vanilla extract
- 1 cup vegetable oil (for frying)
- **For the Chocolate Sauce:**
    - 1/2 cup heavy cream
    - 1/2 cup dark chocolate chips
    - 1 teaspoon vanilla extract
    - 1 tablespoon sugar

**Instructions:**

1. **Make the Churro Dough:**
    - In a saucepan, bring water, butter, sugar, and salt to a boil. Stir in the flour and cook, stirring constantly, until the dough pulls away from the sides of the pan. Remove from heat and allow to cool slightly. Beat in eggs and vanilla until smooth.
2. **Fry the Churros:**
    - Heat oil in a large pot over medium-high heat. Transfer the dough to a piping bag fitted with a star tip. Pipe the dough into the hot oil, cutting it into 3-4 inch lengths. Fry until golden brown, about 2-3 minutes per side. Drain on paper towels.
3. **Make the Chocolate Sauce:**
    - In a small saucepan, heat heavy cream until simmering. Remove from heat and stir in chocolate chips, vanilla, and sugar until smooth.
4. **Serve:**
    - Serve churros with warm chocolate sauce for dipping.

# Poached Pears with Ricotta

**Ingredients:**

- 4 ripe pears, peeled and halved
- 1 cup red wine
- 1/2 cup water
- 1/4 cup sugar
- 1 cinnamon stick
- 1 tablespoon lemon juice
- 1/2 cup ricotta cheese
- Honey, for drizzling
- Chopped pistachios, for garnish

**Instructions:**

1. **Poach the Pears:**
   - In a saucepan, combine red wine, water, sugar, cinnamon, and lemon juice. Bring to a simmer. Add the pear halves and cook for 10-12 minutes, until tender.
2. **Prepare the Ricotta:**
   - In a small bowl, mix ricotta cheese with a drizzle of honey.
3. **Serve:**
   - Plate the poached pears, top with ricotta, and drizzle with additional honey. Garnish with chopped pistachios.

# Lemon Poppy Seed Muffins

## Ingredients:

- 1 1/2 cups all-purpose flour
- 1/2 cup sugar
- 1 teaspoon baking powder
- 1/2 teaspoon baking soda
- 1/4 teaspoon salt
- 2 large eggs
- 1/2 cup milk
- 1/4 cup melted butter
- 1 tablespoon lemon zest
- 1 tablespoon poppy seeds
- 1/4 cup lemon juice

## Instructions:

1. **Prepare the Muffin Batter:**
    - Preheat the oven to 350°F (175°C) and line a muffin tin with paper liners. In a bowl, mix flour, sugar, baking powder, baking soda, and salt. In another bowl, whisk together eggs, milk, butter, lemon zest, poppy seeds, and lemon juice. Combine wet and dry ingredients until just mixed.
2. **Bake the Muffins:**
    - Divide the batter among the muffin cups and bake for 18-20 minutes, or until a toothpick comes out clean.
3. **Serve:**
    - Allow the muffins to cool slightly before serving.

# Sausage and Mushroom Breakfast Casserole

## Ingredients:

- 1/2 pound breakfast sausage
- 1/2 cup mushrooms, sliced
- 1/2 cup shredded cheddar cheese
- 6 large eggs
- 1/2 cup milk
- 1/2 teaspoon salt
- 1/4 teaspoon black pepper
- 1/4 teaspoon garlic powder
- 4 cups cubed bread (stale or toasted)

## Instructions:

1. **Cook the Sausage and Mushrooms:**
    - In a skillet, cook sausage until browned. Add mushrooms and cook until softened.
2. **Prepare the Casserole:**
    - In a bowl, whisk together eggs, milk, salt, pepper, and garlic powder. Combine the sausage mixture with the cubed bread in a greased baking dish. Pour the egg mixture over and top with cheddar cheese.
3. **Bake:**
    - Bake at 350°F (175°C) for 30-35 minutes, or until the eggs are set and golden.
4. **Serve:**
    - Slice and serve warm.

# Baked Avocado with Egg

## Ingredients:

- 2 avocados, halved and pitted
- 4 small eggs
- Salt and pepper, to taste
- Fresh cilantro, chopped (for garnish)

## Instructions:

1. **Prepare the Avocados:**
   - Preheat the oven to 375°F (190°C). Scoop out a small portion of the avocado to create room for the egg.
2. **Bake the Avocados:**
   - Place the avocado halves on a baking sheet and crack an egg into each half. Bake for 12-15 minutes, or until the egg whites are set.
3. **Serve:**
   - Season with salt, pepper, and garnish with cilantro.

# Mango and Coconut Smoothie Bowl

## Ingredients:

- 1 frozen mango, chopped
- 1/2 cup coconut milk
- 1/4 cup Greek yogurt
- 1 tablespoon honey
- 1/4 cup granola
- 2 tablespoons shredded coconut
- 1 tablespoon chia seeds

## Instructions:

1. **Blend the Smoothie:**
    - In a blender, combine mango, coconut milk, Greek yogurt, and honey. Blend until smooth.
2. **Assemble the Smoothie Bowl:**
    - Pour the smoothie into a bowl and top with granola, shredded coconut, and chia seeds.
3. **Serve:**
    - Serve immediately for a refreshing breakfast.

# Sweet Ricotta Croissants with Lemon Zest

## Ingredients:

- 4 croissants, split
- 1 cup ricotta cheese
- 2 tablespoons powdered sugar
- 1 teaspoon vanilla extract
- Zest of 1 lemon
- Honey, for drizzling

## Instructions:

1. **Prepare the Ricotta Filling:**
   - In a bowl, mix ricotta, powdered sugar, vanilla extract, and lemon zest until smooth.
2. **Assemble the Croissants:**
   - Spoon the ricotta mixture into the croissants.
3. **Serve:**
   - Drizzle with honey and serve immediately.

www.ingramcontent.com/pod-product-compliance
Lightning Source LLC
LaVergne TN
LVHW081327060526
838201LV00055B/2502